Virginia,

Merry Christmas! God loves you so much. He gave the best present of all - Jesus! I pray that you will choose to follow Him.

♡ Miss Maria

This book is presented to

Virginia

A gift from

Miss Maria, Miss Heidi, & Miss Katie

On

Christmas 2019

M is for Manger

written by **Crystal Bowman** & **Teri McKinley**
pictures by **Claire Keay**

Tyndale House Publishers, Inc.
Carol Stream, Illinois

Visit Tyndale's website for kids at www.tyndale.com/kids.

Visit Crystal Bowman's website at www.crystalbowman.com.

TYNDALE is a registered trademark of Tyndale House Publishers, Inc. The Tyndale Kids logo is a trademark of Tyndale House Publishers, Inc.

M Is for Manger

Designed by Jacqueline L. Nuñez

Edited by Stephanie Rische

For manufacturing information regarding this product, please call 1-800-323-9400.

ISBN 978-1-4964-0195-3 (hc)
ISBN 978-1-4964-2004-6 (board book)

Printed in China

22	21	20	19	18	17	16
8	7	6	5	4	3	2

To Robby and Nate, my two little miracles.
—C.B.

To Alli, Peyton, Drue, and Brody:
May you celebrate Jesus all year long!
—T.M.

How to Use This Book

The birth of Jesus is one of the greatest miracles in the Bible, and children love to listen to the story every year at Christmas! *M Is for Manger* is the story of that special night when God's Son left his perfect home in heaven to come into this world as a baby. As children turn the pages and follow the letters of the alphabet, the events surrounding the birth of Jesus unfold before their eyes.

The story is told in chronological order, helping young minds understand how and where Jesus was born. They will learn why Joseph and Mary had to go to Bethlehem and how so many of the events of Jesus' birth fulfilled prophecies in the Bible. Bible verses are included with every letter so readers will know where the events or prophecies can be found in Scripture. We recommend reading Luke 2 together as a family during the Christmas season to learn more about the birth of Jesus from the pages of Scripture.

We hope that you and your family will enjoy using this book to focus on the real meaning of Christmas—that God sent his Son to earth to be our Lord and Savior.

Crystal Bowman and Teri McKinley

A is for Angel

An ANGEL said to Mary,
"You are the favored one.
You're going to have a baby boy,
and he will be God's Son."

The angel told her, . . . "You have found favor with God!
You will conceive and give birth to a son."

Luke 1:30-31, NLT

B is for Believed

Mary BELIEVED God's promise,
and in her heart she knew
God had a special plan for her—
the angel's words were true.

You are blessed because you believed that the Lord would do
what he said.

Luke 1:45, NLT

C is for Carpenter

A CARPENTER named Joseph
chose Mary for his wife.
The news that Mary told him
would soon change Joseph's life.

[Jesus] is . . . the son of the carpenter. And his mother is Mary.

Matthew 13:55, ICB

D is for Dream

While Joseph had a DREAM one night,
an angel came to say,
"You can take Mary as your wife
for everything's okay."

While Joseph thought about this, an angel of the Lord
came to him in a dream.

Matthew 1:20, ICB

E is for Elizabeth

Mary knew ELIZABETH
would soon become a mother.
When Mary went to see her,
they were happy for each other.

[Elizabeth said,] "Why am I so honored, that the mother
of my Lord should visit me?"

Luke 1:43, NLT

F is for Family

"It's time to do a census,"
the Roman ruler said.
"Go to where your FAMILY's from—
we'll count you there instead."

[Joseph] went to the town of Bethlehem in Judea . . . because he was
from the family of David.

Luke 2:4, ICB

G is for Gift

Joseph and Mary started out;

they went to Bethlehem.

The greatest GIFT the world has known

would soon be born to them.

Your salvation doesn't come from anything you do. It is God's gift.

Ephesians 2:8, NIrV

H is for Holy

The baby sent from heaven
would be the Lord of all:
the HOLY child, Son of God,
so great and yet so small.

The baby to be born will be holy, and he will be called the Son of God.

Luke 1:35, NLT

I is for Inn

The INN was full in Bethlehem,
so they were turned away.
They found a nearby stable
and slept upon the hay.

There wasn't any room for them in the inn.

Luke 2:7, GW

J is for Jesus

While stars were brightly shining,
JESUS was born that night.
The Son of God came down to earth
to be the saving light.

You are to name him Jesus, for he will save his people from their sins.

Matthew 1:21, NLT

K is for King

Though he was just a baby,
he was born to be a KING.
Jesus will reign forever,
and heaven and earth will sing!

His Kingdom will never end!

Luke 1:33, NLT

L

L is for Love

All along God had this plan
while ruling from above.
He sent his Son to save the world
and show us his great LOVE.

God so loved the world that he gave his one and only Son.

John 3:16, NIrV

M is for Manger

Mary gently wrapped her son,
then rested in the shed.
She placed the newborn Savior
in a MANGER for his bed.

She wrapped [Jesus] snugly in strips of cloth
and laid him in a manger.

Luke 2:7, NLT

N is for Night

This NIGHT was very special.
Soon all the world would know:
the Messiah had been born
who was promised long ago.

The Savior—yes, the Messiah, the Lord—has been born tonight.

Luke 2:11, NLT

O is for Oxen

The shed was filled with animals—
OXEN, cows, and sheep.
They stood around the manger
and watched the Savior sleep.

The Word became human and made his home among us.

John 1:14, NLT

P is for Peace

Some shepherds in a nearby field
saw a brilliant light.
An angel said, "PEACE on the earth.
The Lord is born tonight!"

Glory to God in highest heaven, and peace on earth
to those with whom God is pleased.

Luke 2:14, NLT

Q is for Quickly

The shepherds hurried QUICKLY
like the angel told them to.
And when they saw the baby,
all the things they heard were true.

*[The shepherds] went quickly and found Mary and Joseph with the
baby, who was lying in a manger.*

Luke 2:16, GW

R is for Ruler

When the shepherds saw King Jesus,
they knew he was the one.
Jesus would be the RULER—
God's one and only Son.

O Bethlehem in the land of Judah, . . . a ruler will come from you who
will be the shepherd for my people Israel.

Matthew 2:6, NLT

S is for Savior

God sent his Son to save us,

and that's why Jesus came.

He will be our SAVIOR

if we trust in Jesus' name.

Today in the town of David a Savior has been born to you.
He is the Messiah, the Lord.

Luke 2:11, NIrV

T is for Treasure

When Mary heard the shepherds' words
about her baby boy,
she kept them like a TREASURE
to fill her heart with joy.

Mary kept all these things like a secret treasure in her heart.

Luke 2:19, NIrV

U is for Us

Jesus came for all of US—
his glory filled the earth.
He came to be our Savior
from the moment of his birth.

A child is born to us, a son is given to us.

Isaiah 9:6, NLT

V is for Village

As the shepherds told their story,

they shared it word for word.

The people of the VILLAGE

were amazed at what they heard.

All who heard it were amazed at what the shepherds said to them.

Luke 2:18, NIrV

W is for Wise Men

Some WISE MEN journeyed from the east;
they traveled very far.
They searched and searched for Jesus
by following the star.

After Jesus was born, some wise men from the east
came to Jerusalem.

Matthew 2:1, ICB

X is for Expected

Simeon was a man of God.
He waited long to see
the Messiah he EXPECTED
who would set his people free.

[Simeon] was filled with the Holy Spirit,
and he eagerly expected the Messiah to come.

Luke 2:25, NLT

Y is for Years

Anna was at the Temple
when Jesus came that day.
For many YEARS she stayed there,
to worship God and pray.

[Anna] was now 84 years old. Anna never left the Temple.
She worshiped God by . . . praying day and night.

Luke 2:37, ICB

Z is for Zillions

ZILLIONS of stars shone in the sky,
but one shone big and bright
to tell the world that Jesus Christ
was born on Christmas night.

Where is the newborn king of the Jews?
We saw his star as it rose.

Matthew 2:2, NLT

 # About the Authors

CRYSTAL BOWMAN is a bestselling author of more than eighty books for children, including *The One Year Book of Devotions for Preschoolers, My Grandma and Me, My Mama and Me,* and *The Read and Rhyme Bible Storybook.* She has written many I Can Read! books, as well as stories for *Clubhouse Jr.* magazine and lyrics for children's piano music. She is also the coauthor of *Our Daily Bread for Kids.* Crystal is a mentor and speaker for MOPS (Mothers of Preschoolers), and she speaks at churches, schools, and writers' conferences. Whether her stories are written in playful rhythm and rhyme or short sentences for beginning readers, her desire is to teach children that God loves them and cares for them very much. Crystal and her husband live in Florida and enjoy being grandparents.

TERI MCKINLEY grew up in the world of publishing, attending book signings and book conventions with her mother, Crystal Bowman. She began writing stories in elementary school, and her love for writing grew in college while attending Baylor University. In addition to writing greeting cards for Discovery House Publishers and articles for national magazines, Teri has coauthored several books, including *Our Daily Bread for Kids* and *My Mama and Me.* She has a master's degree in interior design from Arizona State University and enjoys mentoring college students. Teri and her husband live in Texas.

About the Illustrator

CLAIRE KEAY lives in Rayleigh, Essex, United Kingdom, where she colors all day long in her tiny and very messy home studio.

She loves drawing pictures for children (as hard as she tries, she just can't draw "grown-up" pictures), and she spends most of her time illustrating children's books. She also has her own line of digital craft supplies.

Besides drawing and painting, Claire's favorite things are her two beautiful sons, Arsenal Football Club, and breakfast in bed.